How To M**a**ke Money Online

HTeBooks

Copyright © 2016

Copyright © 2016 HTeBooks

All rights reserved. This book or any portion thereof may not be reproduced or used in any manner whatsoever without the express written permission of the publisher except for the use of brief quotations in a book review.

Disclaimer

This book is designed to provide condensed information. It is not intended to reprint all the information that is otherwise available, but instead to complement, amplify and supplement other texts. You are urged to read all the available material, learn as much as possible and tailor the information to your individual needs.

Every effort has been made to make this book as complete and as accurate as possible. However, there may be mistakes, both typographical and in content. Therefore, this text should be used only as a general guide and not as the ultimate source of information. The purpose of this book is to educate.

The author or the publisher shall have neither liability nor responsibility to any person or entity with respect to any loss or damage caused, or alleged to have been caused, directly or indirectly, by the information contained in this book.

Table of Contents

HOW WILL THIS BOOK HELP YOU? 6

WHY YOU NEED EXTRA MONEY 8

THE INTERNET IS A MONEY GARDEN WAITING FOR YOU 10

BEFORE YOU GO FULL THROTTLE: LEARN TO PROTECT YOURSELF 12

VALUE IN THE SMALLEST EFFORTS 16

PAY-TO-CLICK SITES (PTC) 18

PAID SURVEYS 20

SOCIAL MEDIA ADVERTISING 24

GET PAID FOR YOUR REVIEWS 26

TURN PASSION TO PROFIT 28

BLOGGING 30

FREELANCE WRITING 34

E-BOOK PUBLISHING 38

HANDMADE LOVE 42

KICKING THINGS UP WITH KICKSTARTER 44

WHY NOT SELL YOURSELF? 46

TECHNICAL KNOWLEDGE NEED NOT GO TO WASTE 48

WEB INDUSTRY FREELANCING 50

THE ART OF DOMAIN FLIPPING...52

THE ERA OF MOBILE APPS 54

BOOKKEEPING..56

STOCK TRADING 58

LOOK AROUND YOU: OFFLINE ITEMS FOR ONLINE PROFITS 60

IF YOU'RE DONE WITH IT, SELL IT! 62

SPACE IS MONEY 64

NO ERRAND TOO SMALL 66

HOW TO APPLY KEY IDEAS FOR THE BEST RESULTS? 68

How Will This Book Help You?

Money does not make the world go round, but it sure does help to oil its gears. Depending on our living situations, sooner or later there comes a point in our lives when we do realize that money is essential for survival and maintaining the quality of life for us and our loved ones.

Back in the day, society judged those who chased after money as greedy fools, or materialistic people. However, modern living conditions have drastically changed throughout the years, with the gap between the cost of living and wages getting larger and larger with each passing year.

While getting a job is definitely a responsible way to earn money and establish a living, sometimes it's just not enough, and more and more people are realizing that. The internet is fast becoming a great alternative because the only investments you really need are your internet subscription and an inner motivation to earn.

This book will guide you through the vast array of options available and how to make the most out of them. You'll be amazed by the many ways that you can make use of your talent, passion and time to earn extra bucks for you and your family. Some people even turn these into full-time jobs and earn more than their eight-hour office routine! This might just be the break you were looking for. Go on and discover a whole new world of profit!

Why You Need Extra Money

"I have ways of making money that you know nothing of."
– John D. Rockefeller

Tuition fees for the kids, monthly payments for mortgage, bills, car, insurance, not to mention that big vacation coming up for your wedding anniversary, plus the daily allowance of everyone in the house for food, clothing, transportation and other lifestyle needs—these are just some of the things that occupy our budget lists on a daily basis. Most of the time, what we earn with our daytime jobs just isn't enough. As years pass by, the gap between your needs versus income will only grow bigger as the kids get older and as the cost of living rises.

Even if our earnings can supply for our main survival needs, who doesn't want to save a little extra for some treats? And what happens when an emergency arises? Whether we like it or not, having an extra source of income allows the creation of a buffer for unexpected events so as to provide a better sense of security for the family. It also guards your savings against the biggest thief—inflation. Working on having improved cash flow will help you to stand stronger against the rise of prices of daily commodities that slowly but surely eat up an increasing share from your budget.

Making extra money is also a productive way to spend your time and improve your personality. Instead of spending the whole day watching videos of cute dogs and catching up on the latest gossip, working on something you actually like while earning at the same time is obviously a better way to spend your day. Not only does it earn you extra, it also gives you a sense of achievement at the end of the day.

It's not uncommon for people to find themselves in jobs they don't like, forced into it by mere circumstance or the need to survive. It tends to feel depressing because you feel like you're living ho-hum lives with boring routines and awful conditions. Looking for extra work can serve as a great diversion from your day job as you can finally work on things that drive your passion and make you feel alive. The options you'll find in this book will help you decide on where to invest your efforts and your time because yes, there's definitely something for you out there!

Improving your cash flow can affect all areas of your life; do it not just for yourself but also for the people you love.

The Internet is a Money Garden Waiting for You

"Making money is art and working is art and good business is the best art."

– Andy Warhol

The world wide web is a massive network that has seems to penetrate almost every aspect of our lives. We go to social media for keeping in touch with people, YouTube, iTunes, or Spotify, for our daily dose of entertainment, Google for education and random inquiries, Amazon for shopping, and much more! A great number of websites, infographics and articles are set up every day that teach people how to cook, how to talk to their boss, how to grab a date, how to tie their shoes—the internet is now teaching people how to live!

Recent studies show that 2.4 billion people across the world are certified internet users, and the top reasons people have for going online are as follows: research, banking, shopping, meeting people, gaining health information, entertainment and making travel reservations. The internet has managed to make itself relevant in every aspect of life, and people keep consuming everything that it could offer—the good, the bad, the useful and the worthless.

A larger percentage of these users are contented to be in the consuming end of the internet spectrum. These are the people who simply make use of the available services and consume content; but did you know that you can actually move on to the other end and take a better advantage of the online scene?

People favor an increase commerce and industrialization in their own states because it is able to offer more services and more jobs. This goes the same for the internet, as it is fast becoming a commercial super highway for various goods and services. The number of services it offers is proportional to the number of jobs it provides to the people behind it.

On average, 140,000 websites go live each day, so just imagine the number of opportunities this provides to the people behind it! Keep in mind that the extent of its reach is not limited to your town or your country; it actually covers the whole world!

Online jobs are steadily increasing in popularity as the number of people looking for online jobs is matched by the increasing number of companies and individuals who now prefer to out source their services online.

There's surely a spot out there waiting for you! All it takes is for you to find the right opportunities and seize them!

The internet is one of the major commercial, super highways of the world; be sure to take advantage.

Before You Go Full Throttle: Learn to Protect Yourself

"Education is when you read the fine print. Experience is what you get if you don't."

– Pete Seger

The previous chapter has shown you just how huge a market there is for online jobs and services. However, just like in a lot of things in the 'real world', there will always be people who will try to take advantage of the gullible and those who are too eager for their own good. The cloak of anonymity that the internet provides makes these criminals more confident of their evil deeds, and if you are not careful, these people can strip you of your hard-earned cash before you know it. Here are a couple of tips to keep in mind in order to keep yourself safe online.

If it seems too good to be true, it probably is.

This is an age-old mantra for protecting yourself against scammers, and it definitely applies here.

One red alert flag would have to be the 'No experience needed' tag and not providing a set of qualifications. For any job, there should be at least a required skill set or screening process before one is accepted. Unless you're applying for a no-brainer job, do not fall for these antics.

Another would be guaranteeing you thousands of dollars for a week or a month for simply clicking links or doing menial tasks. If you feel that the pay seems way too large compared to the task that you are required, be extra careful as it may be another scam.

Companies that require an advanced fee before you are able to register.

If you really think about it, it doesn't make sense that you have to pay a group so they could pay you. However, these scammers advertise themselves in such a convincing manner that you can't help but think that 'maybe this one is different'—only to find out later on that you just got duped.

Rochelle, a mother of three, was looking for ways to earn online and registered for a translator job and paid a certain fee. It promised a 100% money-back guarantee with zero spam so she gave it a try. After the login, she found the interface too difficult to navigate, and found it hard to look for jobs. Everyone she connected to wouldn't respond, and if they did, they never gave her a job. She decided to get her money back but alas, no one was there to attend to her concerns. In the end, she just got cheated out of $30.

Do not give away your credit card or other financial information via email.

Email is a highly unsafe medium that can be accessed by hackers, phishers and whatnots. There are safer methods to provide payment like PayPal or a sign-in page that shows a padlock icon to indicate security. Always read the address bar to ensure that you are keying in important information on the same website and not on some unsecure pop-up window.

Do not entertain requests from companies you don't know or to complete strangers.

If you don't remember submitting your resume to a particular company, and yet they call you pretending you're they're applicant, be extra cautious and do not give in right away.

Keep your firewall and antivirus software updated.

Companies are making an effort to periodically provide updates that protect your from viruses, malware and trojans that may attempt to steal your information and cause distress. Take time to update these for your own good.

The internet is a huge jungle of opportunities. Protect yourself to make the most out of it.

Value in the Smallest Efforts

"Enthusiasm is the mother of effort, and without it nothing great was ever achieved."

– Ralph Waldo Emerson

Companies spend a great bulk of their budget on advertising, and will go to great lengths just to extend their brand reach and to understand how their consumers perceive their products. This concept has driven an online industry that allows people to earn dollars by doing very simple tasks like clicking links, answering surveys, viewing advertisements and the like. Many people are flocking to this kind of industry because of the promise of earning with very little effort.

As attractive as it is, this type of industry is also one of the most prone to abuse and scams, and must therefore be examined carefully before getting involved. If you feel like the pay is way too large for the equivalent effort required, follow your gut feel and check if it is a scam.

Nevertheless, there are legitimate companies who really use these methods as part of their advertising, and it's a great deal for people who want to earn extra bucks for a couple of minutes. If you can spend a whole hour watching cat videos, then the idea of answering a 15-minute survey for five dollars shouldn't be a bad idea, yes?

Read on to learn more.

No effort is too small for the internet. Everything has value.

Pay-to-Click Sites (PTC)

"Continuous effort—not strength or intelligence—is the key to unlocking our potential."

– Winston Churchill

Clixsense, Probux, Neobux and Fusebux are some of the most trusted online sites when it comes to pay-to-click industries. This is by far the easiest way to earn money in the internet. It basically starts with you clicking the "Register now" button and signing up for their services, then you start to familiarize yourself with the website interface while earning. It will not require you to pay upon registration though some of them may require an optional 'investment' for you to grow your earnings faster, although you'll do just fine even without availing of this option.

The main mechanism of earning is by clicking and watching 30-second ads for and quickly moving on to the next, depending on how much you intend to earn.

Pros: This is the easiest way to earn on the internet, no experience or necessary skill sets are required, and you decide how much time you are willing to allot. They also design the site and advertisements well enough to keep you engaged and entertained during the whole session.

Probux also has a community forum where users can share ideas and help in navigating the site, which makes it all the more legitimate because you are confident that other people are really using and getting paid with it.

These companies also make use of PayPal, Payza, Perfect Money, SolidTrust Pay, and Ego Pay, which allow users to receive their payment without really revealing too much financial information.

Cons: In as much as they provide the easiest ways to earn money, they also have the lowest rates of payment. Clixsense has one of the highest payouts which is $0.02 per click.

These sites also have a minimum payout threshold, meaning you have to accumulate a certain amount before you are able to withdraw to your account. Clixsense has a minimum payout level of $10, which means you'll have to click through the ads 500 times before you are able to withdraw. That's about four and a half hours of viewing ads! As you see, it may take a long while before you are really able to withdraw a substantial amount.

Other sites offer a smaller payout threshold like Neobux that only requires $2, and Probux for only $5. However the rate per click is also lower.

Earning by PTC ads is a great idea only when you intend for this to be an additional activity while browsing the internet. You'll also need to be extra patient with it because it will take a while before you are able to really earn.

Pay-to-click sites offer very low earnings but can still be a great way to spend your time.

Paid Surveys

"Aw, people can come up with statistics to prove anything, Kent. Forfty percent of all people know that."

– Homer Simpson

In any company, the biggest chunk of the budget almost always goes to marketing and advertising. This is because image plays a huge part when making a decision to buy or not to buy a product. Because of this, companies hire the best advertising companies and personnel to ensure that people are aware of their brand and that their customers maintain a positive perception of it.

So how do they know if their advertising and marketing efforts are effective? One method is by growth of sales and purchase behavior, but another more targeted approach is by performing market research.

Market research can be done for two reasons: to learn if a certain marketing strategy is effective or to gain an idea for a future project. A lot of information can be obtained from surveys such as demographics, behavior per age group or location, purchase preference, family background of targeted customers and many more. The standard methods for this type of research involves performing surveys on actual experimental groups. A cheaper and faster way to do this is by conducting paid surveys.

Surveys used to be done for free but companies realized they weren't getting enough volunteers so they decided to pay for it to gain more information. This spurred the growth of hundreds of sites recruiting people to sign up and answer surveys to get paid. This requires a little more effort as compared to PTC sites but it also pays considerably higher. The activity itself is also more entertaining because you get paid by simply expressing your honest opinion.

Some of the popular survey sites include iPoll, Global Test Market, Opinion Outpost, Survey Spot, and National Consumer Panel. All it takes is to look up their webpages and sign up for their services.

Some sites are exclusive only to a particular location like the National Consumer Panel, which is available only to residents of the United States. Survey questions may also be limited depending on your location, age, or industry. This is how companies limit their research participants in order to obtain highly targeted results.

Again take note that the legitimate ones will never ask you to pay for anything before signing up or before receiving any surveys. It is also recommended to join sites that allow withdrawal of points via PayPal, Payza, and similar services in order to protect your financial information. Another tip is to subscribe to several legitimate survey sites at once in order to take advantage of a wide array of markets that require surveys in order to maximize your earnings.

Pros: Answering surveys can be a fun activity for anyone as it allows you to express yourself while earning. It also offers a great insight on the qualities that matter to brands and companies. Some sites can give a $5 incentive for signing up alone, which isn't bad at all. Rates can range from $2 to $50 per survey, though majority of them will be in the $2 to $10 range. If you're really into it, you can spot quality high-paying survey panels that can earn you about $300 in a month.

Cons: One cannot really expect a regular payout for surveys. It depends on the demand and on the category of the individual. Meaning if you're male, you cannot access those that are specifically for women, or sometimes surveys are exclusive to people who belong to certain industries. It can also get tricky to spot high value surveys that have better payouts.

A minimum cash threshold also applies for paid survey sites before you can withdraw your earnings. This can range from $15 to $50. Other sites choose to provide earnings in terms of points, which is in turn convertible to cash. Make sure to compute the equivalent dollar amount of these points for you to have a better idea of their payout rate, as sometimes this can be used to hide the fact that the rate per survey is actually very low.

Taking paid surveys is a fun way to earn, just take time to sort out the best ones and you can actually make decent cash.

Social Media Advertising

"Social media allows us to behave in ways that we are hardwired for in the first place—as humans. We can get frank recommendations from other humans instead of from faceless companies."

– Francois Gossieaux

There are a great many ways to earn money through social media. What we'll discuss for this chapter are the more straight forward methods of making money from your social media accounts.

More than 50% of all internet users all over the world go online for social media. This goes without saying that websites like Facebook and Twitter are huge opportunities for advertising and marketing, and many have taken advantage of the situation by allowing people to earn by displaying advertisements on their profiles.

This is especially profitable for people who have large networks and can be considered 'influencers'. Influencers are those who have a great number of followers and therefore have more powerful recommendations.

Earning can work several ways. Once you display a Facebook ad, you can earn when someone clicks on the link, makes a purchase and leaves their mobile number or email address. Amazon Associates is a great example, though not necessarily limited to Facebook alone. You can display referral links on your timeline and get commissions from sales of your recommended books.

One can also go for paid tweets such as SponsoredTweets.com. As the name suggests, you get paid when your followers click on promotional links via Twitter.

Pros: Displaying Facebook ads can give you around two cents per click, depending on your arrangement with the advertiser. Sponsored tweets can earn you $6 for one tweet for 2000 followers, and can reach up to $1000 for those with a massive following. Given the amount of time that you actually spend on your social media accounts, the rate is fair enough.

A good thing about displaying ads is that you are totally in control of the content that you wish to display. This is also an opportunity to help your followers by making quality recommendations while earning at the same time.

Cons: What seems to work for social media ads can also work against it. Most people really don't like ads, and so coming up with advertising links that are catchy enough to warrant attention may be tricky. Too much hard selling can also turn off some of your followers. It may not be as effective for people who have not yet established a large network of followers.

Social media advertising can be a very lucrative venture, however, it also highly depends on the extent of your social network.

Get Paid for Your Reviews

"You get to make a living; you give to make a life."

–Winston Churchill

Do you remember spending a whole day debating with girl friends on the phone on which makeup was better or what brand of shampoo was the best? Looks like you can actually earn from it!

Again, it all boils down to marketing and advertising. Companies would love to know what you think of their product and are willing to pay you for your opinion.

Vindale Research is an online shopping site that pays you for posting reviews about items that you have bought from their site. You can expect to get paid up to $75 both for answering reviews and surveys on their site. You can make withdrawals via PayPal to ensure security of your information.

Other websites pay you to review other items like User Testing for website interface reviews ($10 per review), Shvoong for reviews about newspapers, academic papers, books and random articles (payout depends on revenue of the product).

Review Stream is another popular pay-for-review website that pays $2 for every review on hot topics and also gives additional points when people rate up your review.

There are a great many legitimate sites that offer payment for each review you give their products; now isn't that a better way to spend all that energy with raving or ranting about various consumer products?

Pay-for-review is another targeted approach for earning extra money. It is a great feedback system that the common consumer can use to reach out to retail companies in order to improve the very products we use.

Getting paid for sharing what you think about your latest purchase seems to be a neat idea, yes?

Turn Passion to Profit

"Pleasure in the job puts perfection in the work."

– Aristotle

"What do you really want to do?"

This is one of the most daunting life questions that hits us some time in our teenage years and stretches up until forever. Some people find the answer sooner, and others never really find out. Circumstances often lead us to doing things that we'd rather not, and necessity tells us that we cannot always do what we want because the cool things don't always bring food to the table.

What if life finally granted you the opportunity to work on what you've always wanted?

The internet is a world without boundaries. It finds value in the smallest of things, rewards your grandest efforts and grants you the possibility of reaching out to all corners of the earth. What may not work in your town may be a hit on a city that is miles away from you. This is a stellar opportunity to finally explore what you've always wanted, feed it to the world wide web and even earn from it! All in the comforts of your home!

Many people have followed their passion and have now gone on to become professional artists, writers, consultants and the like. Do not hesitate to explore your own!

Blogging

"Don't focus on having a great blog. Focus on producing a blog that's great for your readers."

– Brian Clark

Blogging is one of the most common platforms for web content on the internet and can be done by almost anyone. It is a form of social networking that allows you to create your own comprehensive content where you can showcase whatever you wish.

Blogspot and Wordpress are some of the leading blog hosts where people can sign up for free, and it allows anyone to publish their content online. If you have a knack for writing, this one is for you. You can post a wide array of content, from blow by blow accounts of how your day went, reviews of the latest movie you watched, opinion about current events, social commentary, book reviews, advice for mothers, shared experiences about pets and many more. Writing can be done for self-expression or to share experiences that you believe can help other people.

As fun as it sounds, establishing a blog isn't a walk in the park because you will need time and commitment to update it with quality content to keep readers coming back. Junk content that is simply copied from other web pages will easily be disregarded as plagiarized content and will not help the reputation of your site. It is also recommended to find a niche topic that you can focus on so as to target a specific brand of readers and establish a regular following.

A golden rule for web content: quality is king. If your readers find that your website offers something that they cannot easily find with other webpages, they will keep coming back. More readers mean a better reputation for your blog and therefore, higher potential earnings.

Earning through blogging can be done by leasing your webpage space to advertisers, by writing sponsored reviews or blogposts about particular companies, or by selling actual products.

When you gain a following, people keep coming back to your page. The more traffic you get, the more attractive your page becomes to advertisers because they would want to take advantage of your page views and use it to advertise their product.

Using this concept, various sites offer bloggers the ability to display advertising banners on their webpage and get paid for it. There are hundreds of sites that offer these services, and some of the most popular are Infolinks, Sitescout (formerly Adbrite), and Clicksor.

You can get paid from $0.01 to $2 per click depending on the value of the banner. The more traffic you get, the higher chances of people clicking on the banner link, and therefore the more money you get.

Other companies pay for impressions, meaning visitors really don't need to click on the ad for you to earn, they simply have to 'see' it. This has much lower payout rates but is also more convenient to use. Bloggers strategize on the placement of their ads to come up with more clicks and more impressions.

Google Adsense is one of the leading providers of blog advertising. They are the most popular, they provide the highest payouts, but are also the most strict. It is recommended that you purchase a top level domain (www.ebook.com instead of www.ebook.blogspot.com) for them to approve your request. They also go for topnotch quality as all pages with traces of plagiarism or copied content are immediately disqualified. They also strictly screen the nature of content that they approve to ensure that it only provides quality information for potential readers. If one passes through the rigorous screening of Adsense and keeps working on improving their blog quality and traffic, they can expect earnings of $0.15 to $15 per click, with most getting up to $48 for 1000 visits, the highest among all advertisers.

For those who have established a reputation with their blog—if you are a mom known for providing valuable baby-care advice, a girl known for fabulous taste in clothing, or a guy popular among bloggers for keenly observing gadget updates—some companies may want to bank on your influence in the blogosphere by sending you free products to review or by asking you to create a write up about their brand for a fee.

This can be a tricky line to tread however, as some readers may get 'turned-off' when they find that you are being paid by companies to make positive reviews. A good way to work around this is by providing 'full-disclosure' to your readers by telling them if a particular post was sponsored by a brand. You may also want to keep your tone from getting too patronizing to keep your blogger integrity intact. This way, the trust system between you and your reader is maintained. Another great thing about blogging is that the manner in which you create your posts and how you build your reputation is entirely up to you. Therefore, anything that happens is really under your responsibility.

Another great way to monetize your blog is by selling products. You may have some handmade crafts that others may find useful, or a friend who knows a great supplier of accessories and clothing. Instead of renting an actual physical store, you can just post your goodies on your blog, advertise it in your social networking sites and receive orders from people. Selling with this method normally involves having the products delivered to your customers, so make sure that you also know the procedure for shipment.

A lot of people have earned a living by selling online products and relying on social media and word of mouth for their advertising. It's a pretty hassle-free method because your online space is mostly free, and you invest on your product and seller reputation alone.

Amazon Associates can also be used on your blog as you get commissions for every purchase that an item has gotten from your page.

Blogging is a great way to earn money online, but it takes passion and commitment to keep it going because the internet is flooded by all types of bloggers and sometimes it takes a special flair to stand out.

Blogging is not as easy as it seems, but if you've got what it takes, it can also be the most rewarding.

Freelance Writing

"Freelancing is tough. It can be very difficult, in fact. It can wear people down, making them lose sight of what they used to love because they have to do everything else just to get by."

– Mason Hipp

Freelance writing is another way to earn online through the power of the pen—or in this case, the keyboard. Several bloggers venture to freelance writing and vice versa, while a lot of them actually juggle being both. The key difference between blogging and freelance writing is that with the former, you are in full control of the layout and content, and you write for your readers on your terms. Freelance writing on the other hand is pretty much like outsourcing your talent for their purpose, and therefore all articles are written on the client's terms.

It may be easier, or harder, depending on which side of the fence you're on. But freelance writing will definitely give you a more reliable stream of income once you've gotten a hang of it. Beginners can start on sites like Odesk.com or Elance.com, where potential clients and freelancers can meet to discuss terms and gain an interface for communication. The more experienced ones eventually gain contacts of their own and can get projects for higher rates.

Articles can range from simple 400-word description of products or 30-word description of hotels, to 4000-word essays, or long sets of blog posts. Formatting and tone of writing can also vary, which will require flexibility and good writing skills. A strong command of grammar and spelling is a basic requirement, along with the ability to consistently meet deadlines. This also includes the patience required for hours and hours of research.

Freelance writing can be as demanding as a day job or even more. However it still allows you to manage your own time and decide which projects to accept and which to set aside for a later time, as long as you meet the expectations of your client.

Beginners can earn about $30 to $50 an hour, while the more serious ones can earn as much as $80 for an hour and even $2000 for a month.

While these sound like really good money, one must be aware that the life of a freelance writer is anything but easy. Here are a few tips that one should bear in mind when aspiring to become a freelance write.

Get ready for rejections.

Because of the increasing level of competitiveness that this industry requires, one must be ready to experience multiple rejections of their articles. Remember that they are not rejecting you as a person, only your work. Only when you are able to resist from taking rejections personally will you be able to hope to make a living out of freelance writing.

Keep your reputation clean.

Your reputation as a freelancer can either make or break you. Being able to consistently submit deadlines, work according to your agreement with the client and provide quality work are sure-fire ways to boost your chances of being referred to a new clients.

Socialize.

Go out, meet people and socialize. This is another way to develop networks and attract potential clients. Learn to market yourself.

Set your goals.

Are you content with making $1000 a month, or would you like to earn $2000 or more? Set your goals according to your family situation, if you find that you can alot more than 8 hours a day for freelance writing and that you would like to earn a significantly larger amount, then you should go for higher paying clients and better writing gigs.

Seek help.

Hundreds of websites are available for freelance writers who would like to improve their craft or would like to get a hang of the technical matters involved in the trade. Take advantage of these groups in order to meet fellow writers and keep your self motivated.

Self-discipline, persistence and passion are all needed to survive the world of freelance writing. Are you up for the challenge?

E-Book Publishing

"If there's a book to read, but it hasn't been written yet, then you must write it."

– Toni Morrison

If you are a book lover or enthusiast, at one point of your life, you may have dreamed of publishing your own book and being a world-renowned author. You might have sniggered at the thought back then because getting published seemed too far-fetched and ambitious. What if you learned that you can now be a full-fledged author of your own book for real?

The landscape for book-reading has changed quickly since 2012, when e-books outsold hardbound covers for the first time. More and more people have been turning to e-books because of their easy accessibility and portability. In no time, self-published authors gained popularity as well. Digital publishers are making it unbelievably easy for people to publish their own books, and many are taking advantage of this opportunity. Several authors are finding themselves easily selling a thousand e-books a month and are definitely outselling their hardbound counterparts.

If you have an idea sitting in the dark corners of your mind for quite some time, now is the best time to write that e-book, and who knows, it might just give you your first million! Here's a rundown how:

Write.

There's an initial draft that is basically your brain spilled over pages of chaos, a review draft that finally organizes your thought and develops what you really want to say, and the polished editorial draft ready for publishing.

This is of course the most important part of the process because without publish-worthy content, your book will not sell a dime. Focus your thoughts and define your goal straight up—would you like to entertain, to inform or to inspire?

Formatting.

This involves making use of the digital publisher format for your e-book and coming up with a cover. The design of the cover is critical for people to take interest in your e-book. Take note that it also must be attractive even as a thumbnail because that's how your e-book will initially be presented.

A lot of self-published authors try to design their own covers with awful results. It is recommended to hire a professional cover designer to create a more polished look for your book. If you're going to earn thousands of dollars from it, you might as well invest, right?

Publish and Promote.

Head over to your digital publisher, login to your account and follow the pre-defined steps to publish your e-book. You must have your tax info ready for royalties and legality purposes.

Pricing is a very important aspect. Most e-books are priced at $2.99 to $9.99, however, it is found that most readers buy e-books at the $2.99 to $5.99 price range. Price it too high and no one will buy it, but if you price it too low you may not gain enough profit.

There are many digital publishers out there like Nook, iBooks, and Smashwords, however, the leading e-book publisher is Amazon because they have already established themselves as one of the most credible sites for online transactions. The intensive feedback system is top of its class, and they help to extend the reach of your book even to people who have no idea who you are.

Promoting the book is critical to the success of your e-book because no one will buy it if they don't that it exists. Make extensive use of social media, offer incentives for every purchase, or advertise it in online forums and blogs. Take advantage of the digital nature of e-books to spread awareness. It may take a lot of work, but it's definitely worth it.

Publishing e-books is a great way to leave a legacy on your passion or expertise. Now is the best time to do it!

Handmade Love

"That's the thing with handmade items. They still have the person's mark on them, and when you hold them, you feel less alone."

– Aimee Bender

In an era of everything instant and digital, handmade items are regaining their charm and making a comeback. Handmade and custom made items are cool because one knows that they are almost always made with love and are very unique. If you are the kind of person who loves to tinker with things to come up with grand creations, the good news is you can finally sell it somewhere else aside from your garage.

Etsy.com is quite like an indie-store for everything handmade, vintage and awesome. It sells items ranging from paintings, jewelries, accessories, custom-made clothing, vintage toys, craft tools and a whole lot of whatnots. All are vintage, custom-made and lovable. It has created a niche of its own because it can be quite difficult to sell these items on other online shops considering the overwhelming competition with goods that aren't even in the same category. Etsy screens the items that they sell in order to stay true to their niche, making it easier for sellers to find their real market.

Other stores where you can sell handmade goods include BigCartel, Ribbon, and Project Wonderful.

You can of course also use social media to advertise your creations and get orders for them. Facebook pages are now very popular not just for companies but also for independent sellers because of its extensive reach. You can also use your page to advertise garage sales if you insist doing it old school.

Handmade love can actually earn you more love in return. In cash and in kind.

Kicking Things up with Kickstarter

"Chase the vision, not the money; the money will end up following you."

– *Tony Hsieh, Zappos CEO*

In 2009, three people launched an online phenomenon that helped bring back faith in humanity—a crowdfunding venue called Kickstarter. In a nutshell, the creator turns to his audience to fund his project and shares it to them as it launches. It's that simple!

Let's say you had a particularly interesting product, movie, video, book or game in mind; you take the proposal to Kickstarter including the target budget, then you come up with an awesome marketing pitch and finally encourage people to fund your project. All who fund your project will get tangible rewards or experiences in return. Getting more funding means that more people would like to see your project come to life and will pay for it when it is released.

The competition for funding is definitely tight, and so the most successful projects are the ones that capture the imagination of the people and drive innovation.

Since its launch, Kickstarter is known to have launched 135,000 products and gathered up to $1 billion in pledges. Some of its most popular projects are Pebble the smartwatch, Amanda Palmer's album "Theater of Evil," a rare specimen museum, the Veronica Mars movie, a portable 3-D printer pen called 3Doodler, and a hoodie that claims to last ten years. The wide array of projects that can be funded has sparked a flood of innovative ideas as people now have hope that their ideas can come to life even without the backing of huge sponsors.

Similar crowdsourcing groups can be found like Indiegogo and GoFundMe.

Crowdsourcing has its own troubles, as delays in hitting the deadlines may prevent the release of the funds, and failure to follow the strict guidelines may cause disqualification of the project. However, all things considered, it is still one of the most desirable models for launching that big idea that you may have been toying with for quite a while.

Crowdsourcing allows you to dream big with the whole world behind your back.

Why Not Sell Yourself?

"Everyone has talent at 25. The difficulty is to have it at 50."

– Edgar Degas

Before your mind fills with images of a red light district, that is not the kind of selling that you will learn here.

Some people are good in writing, others are master creators, and thus they have products that they can package and sell. But what if your 'product' is yourself? You may be a singer, a dancer, an actress, or a highly reliable consultant or agent. While others may make use of real companies to propel themselves to greatness, the increasing appeal of the internet can help you to package yourself and offer your talents to people armed only by a working internet connection and your wits.

Social media platforms like Facebook and Youtube have been instrumental in making a name out of entertainment greats like Justin Bieber and Boyce Avenue. If you are passionate about performing, then you can take videos of yourself, with the help of friends for production value, and publish it on Youtube. Google Adsense can be displayed on YouTube videos to earn a couple of dollars when viewers click on ads while viewing your video. The competition is stiff as almost everyone has a YouTube account, but the quality of your videos will spell the difference. Of course if your videos go viral, you might even find yourself in TV shows and gain more performing gigs in the future.

Monetizing with Google Adsense can also work for tutorial videos. This is for people who would like to share how-tos to people who are too lazy to read the manual or for other technical matters. In fact, a growing number of lecturers are now uploading their tutorials on YouTube for everyone's consumption. You can also take advantage of this medium to recommend any upcoming book or training session that you may have in order to generate more money.

The way you package yourself is very critical when your selling point is your personal services and talents. Your image must be consistent to your brand and you must be able to utilize all forms of media in order to generate more views and traffic.

There is never a lack for people who pay for great talent. Believe in yourself!

Technical Knowledge Need Not Go to Waste

"Concern for man and his fate must always form the chief interest of all technical endeavors. Never forget this in the midst of your diagrams and equations."

– Albert Einstein

So you earned a bachelors degree, yet you find yourself doing a clerical job. You are raring to go out and put your education to good use because what would all those sleepless nights and sky-high tuition fees be good for? The internet offers an opportunity to make use of your technical knowledge while keeping your current job. That is one of the beauties of freelancing.

There is a great demand for people who are able to breakdown highly technical matters in layman terms or those who are able to provide financial services to people managing small businesses. Since small and medium industries are also on the rise, they would want to outsource some of their highly technical works to freelance consultants who will not charge as high as professional consulting firms. This is a highly targeted market and therefore will have less competition as compared to more general freelancing fields like article writing.

This is also a great opportunity for you to brush up on your technical know-how while earning from your less-challenging-but-higher-paying-job. Once you have established your reputation as a technical freelancer, you may find yourself earning enough to work on it full time.

Read on to find some types of technical knowledge that can be put to use for earning extra money online.

The more specialized your field, the more profitable it becomes.

Web Industry Freelancing

"Content doesn't win. Optimized content wins."

– Li Evans

With almost all stores and transactions now going online, there is a great demand for people who are able to deal with the more technical aspects to securing their online presence. Web professionals are quite like the carpenters, civil engineers and architects of the online world. And so if you have a good command of this field and would like to earn extra online, here are a couple of things you can do:

Create tutorials.

There are alot of web enthusiasts who would love to learn how to set up a website, create a good blog design or deal with servers. One can set up a blog and provide quality and targeted tutorials and earn by blog advertising, or readers can also pay a fee for your expertise. Just make sure that people get what they pay for. Earnings can range from $50 to $150.

Design web pages and blogs.

The design of a website goes beyond what it 'looks like', but also deals with the interface and ease of navigation. It takes technical knowledge to correctly configure these. You can offer these services to aspiring bloggers or start up companies.

Selling templates, patterns and icons.

If you have a great eye for design and love tinkering with patterns and graphics, you can put up some of your designs for sale. Sites like Themeforest allow you to post your original works, and interested users can buy it directly from the site. This is a great way to produce passive income from your creativity.

Keep in mind though that coming up with profitable designs takes years of experience to pull off as it involves an intricate play of shapes, colors and lines.

Finding bugs.

In an era of increasing cybercrime, larger companies are realizing the value of fool-proof software that can prevent hackers from taking advantage of their efforts. Because of this, they offer a hefty amount of cash for people who find vulnerabilities in their codes.

James Forshaw was rewarded $100,000 by Microsoft in 2013 for finding a potential security flaw in one of their softwares. Bugcrowd is a community of similar people specializing in finding coding glitches. It's pretty much a positive reinforcement for people who have incredible skills in order to put their talents to good use instead of resorting to hacking.

There's always been a basis to the saying "Geek is the new sexy."

The Art of Domain Flipping

"Everyone lives by selling something."

– Robert Louis Stevenson

Think of 'domains' as addresses to a house. This refers to the site address of your webpage like www.ilovethisebook.com for example. However, to get this address for yourself, you will have to buy it from web host and domain providers so you could own it. This prevents someone else from the opposite side of the world from putting up a page named www.ilovethisebook.com because that domain name is already yours.

So what if you have gotten so successful and realized that you would like to rename your site to www.ilovethisebooksomuch.com? You will have to buy this domain again and leave your former webpage address to expire. This will allow the happy lady from the opposite side of the world to finally own a website named www.ilovethisebook.com.

Domain flippers work in between these transactions to make profits. You can go through a list of unregistered domain in sites like GoDaddy and look out for expired domain names that may be of great value for someone you know. You can purchase www.ilovethisebook.com for about $70, then send an email to a happy lady who would gladly pay you $200 for it. Bravo! The profit is made!

The key in earning through this method is being observant of current trends and insightful for things that may spark interest among people, purchasing domains while their value is still low, then selling it at a great price when you find it most profitable.

It definitely involves risk as you may encounter having to sell domains for zero profit. However the rewards you get in the process may make this worth a try.

Domain flipping is pretty similar to buying and selling real estate properties.

The Era of Mobile Apps

"Every man is a creative cause of what happens, a primum mobile with an original movement."

– Friedrich Nietzsche

The smartphone and tablet market is now saturated with apps of all shapes and sizes. While smartphone designs and capabilities are all the craze right now, mobile apps are quickly catching up because they allow you to use your phone for several functionalities that the manufacturer wasn't able to include.

There's an app that measures your heart rate, an app that reads your horoscope for the day, an app that gives directions, an app that plays dice and not to mention the gazillions of games that are available both in Android's Playstore and Iphone's Appstore. The most successful of apps are known to be earning thousands of bucks per month out of user purchases, and believe it or not, Candy Crush is actually earning $947,000 every day. Incredible!

What attracts alot of people is that it is open to everyone with the right amount of tools and knowledge. In spite of the saturated market, people still love to create something that others can use or have fun with, quite similar to publishing e-books. And there's always that hope of being the next viral thing and waking up a millionaire the next day. Remember Flappy Bird?

Creating a mobile app entails a complicated web of wire framing, data integration, user-interface development and design, server-side logic and user management among others. But the bottom line is to create an app that can delight, entertain or be greatly useful for specific applications.

The interface of the app must be designed in an appealing and engaging manner following the modern laws of design and user-friendliness. It has to be comprehensively tested and refined with zero to minimal bugs.

Android will let your apps launch untested in the Playstore while iPhone requires all apps to undergo a review process that takes about a week. Once it's out there, your apps will be tested through user reviews and purchases.

One thing that developers forget though is to advertise their apps. This is essential if you really want to earn.

Mobile apps are the next best thing to coming up with your own custom made gadgets, do you agree?

Bookkeeping

"Accounting does not make corporate earnings or balance sheets more volatile. Accounting just increases the transparency of volatility in earnings."

– Diane Garnick

Another technical skill that could be put to use is bookkeeping. This basically entails keeping a clean record of all the cashflow details of a particular company or individual. This includes keeping track of all invoice, receipts, earnings and payables. This is gaining increasing momentum in several countries because more and more entrpreneurs are trying to enter businesses without knowing how to streamline their cashflow. This is critical to businesses because it allows you to keep track of your collectibles and your deadlines. Unmanaged finances will only cost a business more money and bad reputation in the future.

This type of industry is good for people who don't get bored with numbers, have an eye for detail and an integrity to keep records clean. Various online courses are now being offered for people who would like to get a hang of the industry, but one may require a couple of years of actual training before gaining enough reputation to work as an independent bookkeeper.

Armed with sufficient storage, reliable accounting software, and a great ability to organize, bookkeeping can be a great work-at-home job for people. The average bookkeeper earns $25 to $40 per hour but can also increase depending on work load and location.

Adding tax preparation services can also increase your value as a bookkeeper, and so does an accounting background. Having business cards and referrals from former satisfied clients will also boost your reputation.

Bookkeeping lets you use your love for numbers to save someone else's business.

Stock Trading

"Price is what you pay. Value is what you get."

– Warren Buffett

If you find yourself with more saved cash and an appetite for risk, stock trading may a good venture for you. To put it simply, stock trading involves buying shares of certain companies for a particular price, then selling them afterwards for a profit when the value of these companies rise.

While it does sound easy, a comprehensive research must be done before one engages in stock trading as it's not uncommon for people to lose their hard-earned money when the economy stumbles and the prices of companies suddenly crash. Smarter traders can get profits of as much as 600% in three years, but this is backed by long years of experience and 'feel' of the stock market.

Here are a couple of tips to earn extra money from stock trading.

Be in it for the long haul.

Patience has always been a virtue, and the same holds true for stock trading. You will need to learn to apply the "buy at the low and sell at the high" law, and it requires alot of patience to keep yourself from buying just because everyone else is buying because chances are the price may be a little too high, and it will affect your profits.

You also cannot expect a 30% profit right away in your first year of trading, as it may take five years for you to truly realize your profits.

Buy great companies.

One of the things that make stock trading a hit is the fact that your earnings depend on how well your company performs. That being said, a great deal of research must be done on a company before you decide to buy a piece of it. Does it have a good management team? Does it have years of experience to show for it's stability? How profitable is it? Many experienced investors say that you should only buy a company that you truly know about for you to understand how it will be affected by key events.

Diversify.

Another good tip is to not keep your eggs in the same basket. Do not focus all your investment on a single company to keep yourself from crashing with it when unexpected events take place. It is always a good practice to invest in various industries to create a buffer of your investments.

Stock investing is for the bold of heart.

Look Around You: Offline Items for Online Profits

"The most unprofitable item ever manufactured is an excuse."

– John Mason

Think all the previous ideas in this book are too hard for you? The following chapters will lead you to finding more ways to earn good cash online without having skill sets or talents required.

How could this be possible? Well look around you. That old china from your great-grandparents. Do you really need that? You think someone else would love it?

How about that extra room that no one's been sleeping in for the past ten years because your son has already moved out of the house? Would you mind 'renting' it out?

Or would you mind buying a random stranger a cup of coffee?

The outrageous connectivity that the internet allows us also brings forth great innovative ways for people to earn money by performing the most mundane tasks. Go on and read about these novel ideas!

Once again, no effort is too small for the internet.

If You're Done With It, Sell It!

"Salesmanship is limitless. Our very living is selling. We are all salespeople."

– James Cash Penney

One of the things that we have to deal in life is clutter. No matter how we try to clean and reorganize, life just has a way of filling our houses with so much clutter we can hardly move. Sometimes clutter is related to the personality of the owner, as the more sentimental ones are less likely to let go of their old items.

Decluttering your room feels like decluttering your own life and is highly recommended especially for people who are going through rough patches for its therapeutic effect. A very profitable way of going about this is to actually sell your pre-loved items over at the internet. Well if you could actually earn from it, then you wouldn't need to go through periods of drama just to get rid of junk, right?

Amazon , e-Bay and Craiglist are some of the most popular sites to sell your second hand goodies. To maximize your profits, you wouldn't want to just throw it over the web. Here are some tips that you may want to keep in mind:

Sort your clutter to things that are plain garbage, worthless and those that may have a considerable resale value. Does it work? Is it intact except for a few millimeters thick of dust? No matter how old it is, someone out there may make good use of that.

Take note of the pricing. Check out how much it costs brand new, how much it costs used and then base your pricing from there. Restoring the item to a good condition may allow you to add a couple of dollars to the price.

Gadgets and electronics are best sold in the Amazon Marketplace. The same goes for home appliances. Just keep track of the cut that Amazon may take during pricing, as it can be pretty steep.

Textbooks can also be sold in Amazon Marketplace and Ebay, but more targeted buyers can be found at Chegg and Half.com.

Do not forget to keep in mind shipping costs during pricing, and ensure to keep your goods in good condition prior shipment. On time delivery and quality will improve your reputation as an online seller.

Sometimes the best way to let go is to find your treasure a new owner.

Space is Money

"Come live in my heart, and pay no rent."

– Samuel Lover

To again prove that you need not look far to make money, several people are now discovering that they can go online to offer their spare rooms for people who cannot afford to rent hotels. Airbnb is one of the leading sites offering this service, and if you do have a spare room, you might just make money out of this one. This is profitable for people who live in the city or in known tourist destinations and is another way to earn passive income for rent without necessarily purchasing a brand new home.

However, online renting can be risky for users because the actual scenario may turn out differently from what was agreed on their lease. Airbnb tries it's best to provide safe transactions between lessor and lessee, however, this is still the internet, and sometimes people just can't keep their word. This is where the feedback system helps alot, in order to warn people of unpleasant incidents and the like. Here are a couple of tips to ensure a good reputation as a host and gain more earnings from leasing your space online.

Grant your guests complete information.

Directions on how to get to your place, or even tips to the must-see places, give plus points to you as a host.

Keep it tidy.

Guests would want to see their room just the way they saw it in the internet, so cleanliness and tidiness is a must. A trashbin for their use would also be appreciated.

Comfortable rooms.

It's very stressful to find yourself rushing to the bathroom in the middle of the night only to realize that it's too disgusting to use and does not have a tissue. Simple things like this make all the difference to a guest.

Guest space.

Your place may not be a hotel, but you're still making a business out of accomodations, so at the very least you may want to designate their space in the kitchen, the fridge and make sure that they're comfortable.

Transparency.

If you are going to convince anyone to live on your place, you first have to show them that you can be trusted. This can be achieved by using a legitimate photo for your profile and listing down as many items as possible about your room for rent to paint a complete picture.

Safety.

You are allowed to refuse guests if you're not comfortable about them. At the end of the day it's still your place, and you have the right to protect what's yours.

You can also find spaces for rent on Craiglist and other websites. Park In My House and Park Let are similar services that rent out parking spaces instead of rooms.

Renting out space can be a great way to maximize your home and earn passive income.

No Errand Too Small

"Happiness lies in the joy of achievement and the thrill of creative effort."

– *Franklin D. Roosevelt*

The last in our list deals with something so mundane but is very much a part of our daily lives—errands. These are the small tasks that we need to accomplish regularly to keep a household or a sane life going. With an increasingly fast-paced world however, some people find themselves too busy with their schedules to even care about cleaning their house, paying their bills, fixing their faucet or the like. These people are actually willing to pay for someone else to do it so they could move on to more things that are way up in their priority lists.

That's where you come in; he get's his errands done while you walk away with extra money. Everybody happy! This trend is also becoming a hit among elders who need extra help to go about their daily activities.

The average pay for this service is about $20 to $40 per hour. Some errand-runners can even earn as much as $200 a day for these. Another good thing about it is the fact that gaining good reputation as an errand-runner can also earn you referrals for higher paying jobs.

Websites like TaskRabbit provide a place where potential employers and errand-runners meet and negotiate. However, this is still limited to cities in the United States. Even if you do not live in these areas, you can still post the services you offer in social media sites or via Gigwalk.

Beyond the triviality of these tasks, it is the fact that you are able to help others carry on with their lives that make these gigs interesting.

How to Apply Key Ideas for the Best Results?

The possibilities for earning on the internet are practically endless. Depending on your personality and interest, one or more of these options will surely work for you. Go on and explore!

Look up websites that reward small tasks like pay-to-click, pay-to-review and paid surveys. Compare rates, user interface and customer feedback to filter through hundreds of options. Once you have signed up for three to five sites, make it a habit to allot at least 15 to 30 minutes per day to view ads and answer surveys. These may give significant earnings at first, but your daily efforts will eventually accumulate to something more.

Exercise your writing muscles; start up a blog! This is a great way to reacquaint yourself with the idea of regular writing, and once have brushed up on your grammar, skill and the various formats of web content, you can start signing up for freelancing sites and explore the world of freelance writing. Who knows; you may even move on to write your very first e-book!

Come up with a list of your talents and activities that you love doing. If you have some hidden masterpieces in your bedroom that you think could make some cash, take a good photo of it and post it on Etsy.com. Or maybe take a video of yourself grooving to the latest dance craze. It may feel silly, but hey, just have fun!

If you are equipped with technical training from various fields, try to look over at Elance.com or Odesk.com and check out people who might be looking for people of with your qualifications. Help them solve their problems, and you might just enjoy earning from it.

Look around you and sort out some valuables that you no longer use. You might just earn a huge amount from disposing all those dusty furniture and appliances that you never use anyway.

Help people out. It's not bad to ask for a fee for helping especially when you're asked to do it regularly, and you're not over-charging anyway. It might even pave the way to bigger and better gigs!